Disruptive Mood Dysregulation Disorder (DMDD), ADHD and the Bipolar Child Under DSM-5:

A Concise Guide for Parents and Professionals

Dr. Todd Finnerty
Psychologist

Published by PsychContinuingEd.com, LLC
Columbus, Ohio

Disruptive Mood Dysregulation Disorder (DMDD), ADHD and the Bipolar Child Under DSM-5: A Concise Guide for Parents and Professionals, by Todd Finnerty.
ISBN 0981995527, ISBN-13: 978-0-9819955-2-6
1. Psychology 2. Parenting

Correspondence may be sent to:
Todd Finnerty, Psy.D.
e-mail: toddfinnerty@toddfinnerty.com
Twitter @DrFinnerty

Publisher- Columbus, OH: PsychContinuingEd.com, LLC (also known as WorldWideMentalHealth.com)
First Edition, First Printing
100 E Campus View Blvd, suite 250
Columbus, OH 43235

In less than 10 years the rate that children are diagnosed with bipolar disorder increased a shocking 4000%! This was due in part to the increased use of "alternative," unsanctioned approaches to making the diagnosis in children. As more research has been conducted and we've gained more experience with "the bipolar child," it turns out that most don't grow up to have bipolar disorder and they're distinctly different from the much smaller number of children who really do have bipolar disorder. These kids not only have not had an "early onset" of bipolar disorder, they haven't had an onset of bipolar disorder at all. We must move forward with better research and better approaches to treatment. These children can't afford for us to cling to unsupported diagnoses. Under DSM-5 most of these kids are now better suited for the new DSM-5 diagnosis of Disruptive Mood Dysregulation Disorder (DMDD).

DMDD is a unipolar (not bipolar) mood disorder characterized by very severe irritability. Any parent of a DMDD child can tell you that their problems are not simply normal, developmentally appropriate "temper tatrums." Kids with DMDD are already in need of treatment, they're just not getting the best treatment that they could be. DMDD shares qualities with ADHD and ODD but also reflects substantial emotional concerns as severe as any bipolar disorder. In this book Dr. Finnerty confronts the popularized notion of "the bipolar child" and offers resources and "less toxic" advice for parents and professionals.

Table of Contents

Introduction and History of early-onset bipolar disorder and the DSM-5's DMDD... 6

The Bipolar Child (throw out this book)... 20

The Disruptive Mood Dysregulation Disorder Diagnostic Criteria... 33

Do adults have DMDD? ... 37

What diagnostic code should Disruptive Mood Dysregulation Disorder be billed under in DSM-5? ... 40

What Changes have been made to Bipolar Disorder in DSM-5? ...42

Differential Diagnosis and Comorbidity: Is it DMDD, a "Bipolar Child" or some other problem? ...44

Changes to ADHD, ODD and other childhood disorders in DSM-5... 55

Treatment options, Measuring Outcomes & Parenting the DMDD Child...58

For further reading: Parents...76

For further reading: Professionals ...77

Continuing Education Credits for this book are available at www.*PsychContinuingEd.com*

Subscribe to DMDD news today
FOR FREE

www.disruptivemooddysregulation.com/DMDDnews

Introduction and History...

Over the last decade and a half some professionals have argued that a group of children and adolescents with significant problems were not getting the attention that they deserve by researchers and clinicians. Some of them also argued that these children should be called "bipolar." Unfortunately, they were only half right-- they shouldn't be viewed as "bipolar."

I'm Dr. Todd Finnerty and I'm a clinical psychologist in Columbus, Ohio. The purpose of this book is to be useful and informative for both mental health professionals and an interested general audience of parents, teachers and patients. I'm not an ADHD, bipolar disorder or DMDD researcher-- I'm a clinician. As a licensed psychologist who has worked with kids who meet the diagnostic criteria for DMDD, I find the development of new approaches for these kids encouraging. I'm hopeful for a better future for our treatment of them. You can also find more resources by visiting my website at www.toddfinnerty.com

Many terms have been in use to refer to these children who have been treated as though they were bipolar kids. The disorder has been referred to as child bipolar, pediatric bipolar disorder, early-onset bipolar disorder, juvenile mania and more.

Currently kids that meet the criteria for DMDD are already being identified for treatment. They are getting diagnoses like Bipolar Disorder NOS as well as multiple diagnoses at the same time like ADHD, ODD and learning disorders. While the central focus of this book is on DMDD, we'll also address some ADHD issues since many of the kids with DMDD will meet at least some of the ADHD criteria. In the book we discuss ways of deciding whether a problem is just "normal" temper tantrums or if it is ADHD, DMDD or both. In terms of Oppositional Defiant Disorder (ODD), professionals should not diagnose ODD & DMDD together (professionals will just diagnose DMDD since DMDD is more severe than ODD).

In writing this book I have attempted to avoid unnecessary jargon while still respecting that parents and teachers are smart enough to tackle these topics. In addition, the material is in-depth enough to qualify for continuing education for mental health professionals and they can get CE credits for reading this book by going to www.psychcontinuinged.com. However, the book is not designed to offer an extensive review of the research literature. It primarily focuses on popular claims in the press and presents an alternative view which is more consistent with the current research and current approach taken by DSM-5.

Understanding the recent history of pediatric bipolar disorder is important to understanding why we now have a DMDD diagnosis under DSM-5.

In less than 10 years (from 1994 to 2003) the incidence of children diagnosed with bipolar disorder increased 4000%! That means that dramatically more youths were being diagnosed with bipolar disorder than had been previously. This dramatic increase is partially a result of "looser" interpretations of the criteria for diagnosing bipolar disorder that were advocated by some professionals. Multiple different research criteria were created that were different depending on which researcher you talked to. These various, competing research criteria served to create a climate of confusion and non-evidenced based clinical practice outside of a solid research base. It also captured the media and the public's attention and made early-onset bipolar disorder a frequently discussed topic. There was no officially agreed upon diagnostic criteria for a "child-version" of bipolar disorder despite the fact that various researchers and authors promoted their own versions to the public. There is no new DSM-5 early-onset/pediatric bipolar disorder diagnosis either. While some changes have been made to diagnosing bipolar disorder in DSM-5, there is no uniformly accepted way to diagnose a "bipolar child" except by using the same criteria that is used with adults. In fact, changes have been made in DSM-5 to make it even *less* likely that the child envisioned as a "Bipolar Child" in some popular books gets diagnosed with bipolar disorder in DSM-5. A new diagnosis has been created and changes have been made to the Bipolar I diagnosis to this end. It is important for parents and professionals to understand why.

Multiple research groups have been working on the question of bipolar disorder in children and adolescents and these groups sometimes used different research criteria and different interpretations of what qualifies as mania and what qualifies as bipolar disorder in children. This makes evaluating their research and comparing it to other groups difficult at times. The debate continues about whether there is a "developmental manifestation" of bipolar disorder in children that looks differently than what bipolar disorder looks like in adults; however the expert consensus achieved by those framing DSM-5 is that the evidence does not sufficiently show that there is. There is also debate on how to classify adults who are sometimes diagnosed with bipolar disorder NOS despite a lack of a cyclical presentation. That means that their problems do not tend to differ significantly from time to time depending on what point in a bipolar cycle they happen to be. However, many now agree that most of the children diagnosed with bipolar disorder have significant difficulties but do not actually have a disorder that is related to what we've classically viewed as bipolar disorder. When these alternative views of early-onset bipolar took hold there was not a lot of good research available on these kids. Much more research is now "in." While diagnosing many of these children as having a bipolar disorder has become popular and has made some professionals' careers, that does not mean it has become scientifically-supported.

To say that "pediatric bipolar disorder" has become a popular diagnosis that has received a lot of media attention is an under-statement. Over the last two decades there has also been a sharp increase in the research being done on children and adolescents who may have bipolar disorder. The controversy about whether some kids have bipolar disorder, often diagnosed under DSM-IV as Bipolar Disorder NOS (not otherwise specified), has not gone away. While a relatively small number of these kids do have bipolar disorder, many have been diagnosed as a bipolar child when in fact they will not go on to display the symptoms of bipolar disorder when they are adults. Children are right now being called "bipolar" even though they don't meet the DSM-IV or DSM-5 criteria for that diagnosis. These children are being called "bipolar" even though they don't grow up to have classic bipolar disorder as adults. They are however, more likely to grow up to have unipolar depression and other concerns. It seems strange to call a child "bipolar" when that child doesn't meet the criteria for bipolar disorder and that child likely won't grow up to develop bipolar disorder as an adult. It seems strange to call a child "bipolar" when research has shown them to be dramatically different from what we would typically refer to as bipolar. It

seems potentially harmful to give a child
a diagnosis that implies life-long
impairment when the research does not
support that these kids will have bipolar
disorder all of their life. It seems
potentially harmful to give them a
diagnosis which could unnecessarily
impact their ability to get certain jobs in
the future. It seems unwise to label these
children with a diagnosis that suggests a
life-long prescription for toxic
medications as opposed to intervening
with psychotherapy and potentially less
toxic medications. That is why there has
been a focus on these children with mood
dysregulation and severe irritability.
Children with DMDD are not simply kids
with a developmentally appropriate level
of temper tantrums. They are not just
kids who are temporarily dealing with
significant stressors in their environment.
These children clearly need help—some of
them are even being hospitalized.
However, we must be sure they are
getting the most appropriate help. These

kids shouldn't be treated as though they have bipolar disorder, but making diagnoses in children is difficult and sometimes tentative.

It is important to remember that bipolar disorder presents in discrete episodes. That means that a child may seem normal sometimes and have specific periods of time when they have mania, hypomania and depression. Ellen Leibenluft, MD and her lab group have also researched individuals they termed as experiencing "severe mood dysregulation." This is a more chronic form of irritability in kids who often meet the criteria for multiple diagnoses including ADHD, Oppositional Defiant Disorder (ODD), specific learning disabilities and language impairment. Severe mood dysregulation was originally developed as a for-research bipolar "phenotype," or a way to reflect what many professionals were theorizing that some bipolar children looked like. The severe mood dysregulation concept was designed as a way to research whether bipolar disorder really did look differently in children than in adults. However, the evidence from these researchers at the NIMH actually led us away from concluding that these children had bipolar disorder.

Leibenluft's research has found that these children are distinctly different groups than the "classically" bipolar children. Research has found that these children do not go on to have bipolar disorder as adults. This research is the foundation for the new diagnosis in DSM-5, Disruptive Mood Dysregulation Disorder (DMDD). DMDD is not for kids with normal temper tantrums. These children have severe, non-episodic irritability which creates significant impairment and a need for intervention. This means that their irritability tends to be relatively constant. While they may not constantly be having "outbursts," they tend to constantly be at risk for them and not just "episodically" fluctuating between periods of depression, periods of normal moods and periods of mania. Over the last decade children with severe, non-episodic irritability have increasingly been labeled "manic," but they've been labeled manic in error.

Is it a tantrum, outburst of rage or a manic episode? We should never "diagnose" mania based on only one symptom—especially not irritability. Irritability is much like a fever as it can mean many things. However, many times children may receive a bipolar disorder NOS diagnosis primarily due to those behavioral concerns resulting from irritability. The work of Leibenluft and others has led to the DSM-5 proposed new diagnosis of Disruptive Mood Dysregulation Disorder (originally proposed as Temper Dysregulation Disorder with Dysphoria) to classify a group of individuals with chronic irritability that do not have the episodic quality of bipolar. Some critics have argued against Disruptive Mood Dysregulation Disorder because they don't want to pathologize "temper tantrums." These critics clearly have an agenda as they've said that DMDD is an excuse to medicate toddlers, but the diagnosis can't even be made in toddlers due to the age limits in the diagnostic criteria. These critics have disregarded the fact that DMDD cannot be diagnosed until age 6, after the time where frequent temper tantrums are more common developmentally (though very few children tend to experience the frequency of "normal" temper tantrums they'd need to be confused with DMDD). Children qualifying for the DMDD diagnosis experience significant, developmentally inappropriate difficulties and these so-called "tantrums" are so bad that they are being mischaracterized as "manic" by some professionals. Their so-called "normal" temper tantrums are leading them to be psychiatrically hospitalized.

However, children who meet the criteria for DMDD are erroneously being diagnosed with bipolar disorder and are being medicated as though they have bipolar disorder. Viewing children without bipolar as though they were bipolar leads them down the path of incorrect treatments including medications that may be more toxic than necessary (ex: antipsychotics) and may also lead parents and professionals to inaccurately view them as expected to have bipolar disorder for the rest of their life. The research shows that this simply isn't accurate. Trying to pass off DMDD as normal "temper tantrums" is akin to calling a severe depression just "the blues." However, it also isn't bipolar disorder.

While there are other disorders of childhood that can be diagnosed in these children like ADHD, Depression and ODD, the reality is that the pediatric bipolar disorder rate increase was fueled in part by the lack of any appropriate "diagnostic home" for these children and adolescents. DMDD therefore serves a very useful purpose and the continued research and recognition of this population is very important to ensure that this group of children is not being "overmedicated" or routed to improper treatments.

The Bipolar Child (throw out this book)

Even if the DSM was "psychiatry's bible" it shouldn't always be interpreted literally. Professionals can go too far in stretching creative interpretations of the DSM, however. One such instance of creative interpretation causing trouble is with the concept of early-onset bipolar disorder. Alternative approaches also began being referred to as "bibles" by marketers even though the research on such approaches was tenuous. Books like *The Bipolar Child* from Demitri Papolos, MD and Janice Papolos should not be considered "the bible" on Bipolar Disorder any more. These books shouldn't be considered the bible on anything. The approach to "pediatric bipolar" in many of these books cast far too wide a net and include many different childhood problems under one umbrella. They lump too many kids with different problems all together under the same, unfortunate and incorrect label of "bipolar." These kids need to be recognized by professionals. These kids need to be studied. However, these kids do not necessarily have a bipolar disorder.

It may be unfair to single out just one book and use it as a symbol of a wider trend like the dramatic increase in bipolar diagnoses in children. It is not my intention to create an "Oswald" or a scapegoat that suggests that any one of the many books on bipolar kids caused the commotion—they did not. However, I think reviewing one of these as a patsy is educational and informative. It will also hopefully begin to help dispel the myths and misinformation that has quickly become pervasive about these kids.

One early and influential book, first published in 1999, has seen multiple editions. It's titled *The Bipolar Child* and is by Demitri Popolos, M.D. and Janice Popolos. When the book first came out advocating for these kids to be called "bipolar" there was very little known compared to what we know now. The book and other efforts like it did much to help call attention to *groups* of children and adolescents who need more research attention and more help than our system was giving them.

However, "The Bipolar Child" and many publications like it have now outlived their usefulness and the current editions should be thrown away and disregarded. These books are now more dangerous than they are informative.

The advice in these books is not only not revolutionary at all, they are not consistent with the current state of the field and may potentially lead parents and professionals in the opposite direction from good treatment and good diagnostic practices. They began being written even before we had much research evidence and are now promoting diagnostic practices which are inaccurate and inconsistent with the research evidence we now have. In fact, *The Bipolar Child* continues to cite more of the authors' online surveys than it describes good research. It's not clear if the author (researcher) even independently examined the children in some of the reported e-mail surveys himself to verify whether they actually even had his proposed version of bipolar disorder.

If you read books like *The Bipolar Child* you'll soon discover that nearly every childhood problem imaginable becomes diagnosable as bipolar disorder. It seems that the authors cast an ever wider and wider net in which to ensnare as many children with problems as possible under the "bipolar" label. However, "early-onset bipolar" is a misnomer for many of these children. It suggests that there has actually been an onset of bipolar when there has not been.

 If you read books like *The Bipolar Child* you'll soon discover that it's far too great a risk to treat kids with any medication that might trigger "mania," and therefore the safest thing to do is to treat them with even more toxic drugs that are not even FDA approved for use in children. These conclusions are dangerous and books like this should be removed from your shelf. They offer too many misleading and even sometimes inaccurate themes. The advice given related to medications leading to mania, while grounded in some fact, is presented in a way that could in fact be "toxic" to your child.

Some of the concerning themes from *The Bipolar Child* are noted here in italics (with quotations being direct quotes from the book itself):

> *Bipolar disorder in children "presents very differently from how it presents in adults" and "requires its own criteria."*

This is not accurate and not supported by current research. In fact, not only is this inconsistent with research from Dr. Ellen Leibenluft's group at the NIH, it is not consistent with the conclusions reached by the professionals forming DSM-5. This is one reason why the new diagnosis, DMDD, was included in DSM-5. While these kids do require their own diagnostic criteria, it's not bipolar disorder criteria.

"The majority" of bipolar children cycle rapidly from depression to mania and back again. Some "cycle over a period of days; others seem to alternate mood states several times throughout the day."

Some of these children may not actually be experiencing mania but a more persistent, severe irritability which is not actually the same thing as a manic episode. It may benefit from different forms of treatment. A thorough evaluation from a child psychologist or other competent professional is recommended.

"While mixed states are not as common in adults unless induced by antidepressant treatment, they are a hallmark of the ultrarapid cycles found in childhood-onset bipolar disorder."

Interestingly, while Dr. Papolos noted believing that "mixed states" are the *"hallmark"* of childhood-onset bipolar disorder, the DSM-5 *eliminated* the "mixed type" Bipolar I Disorder. The DSM-5 actually reduced the use of these "mixed" episodes where depression and mania symptoms are present at the same time. It does allow for a specifier, however, in the event that mania or depression presents with some of the symptoms of the other. However, while rapid cycling is generally around 4 times per year, these ultra-rapid proposals that occur within the same day should be viewed with significant caution.

Bipolar Disorder is far more common than was previously supposed

As it turns out, "classic" bipolar in children exists but it is still relatively rarer compared to the rate of children being diagnosed with these broad, less-supported approaches.

> Treatment with mood stabilizers should be considered a "first line" approach instead of less toxic medications like antidepressants or stimulants because of the potential risk of triggering a manic episode.

There is some truth to concerns related to potential increased suicide risk with antidepressants. There is some truth to concerns about potentially triggering manic episodes. However, one conclusion that should be reached is that psychotherapy should be considered for many of these children and their families. In addition, a comprehensive history and evaluation to rule out actual mania should be conducted. It should be concerning that children who have only shown irritability or have only shown signs of a unipolar disorder are subjected to more toxic medications as a "first line" option on the speculative notion that a manic episode could be triggered and that the irritability that they are showing is mania. It's even more concerning because these medications have not been fully demonstrated to be safe and effective in kids as they are not FDA approved for children. This is one reason why, as a psychologist, I'd suggest you also seek advice from a good child psychologist regarding psychosocial interventions.

> "Some bipolar children are so sensitive to stimuli that they cannot tolerate pockets in clothing or labels or collars on shirts." They have difficulties making transitions.

It's possible that "some" do. Children have many unique concerns. However, sensitivity to stimuli and/or difficulties making transitions can be found in many other childhood problems including ADHD, anxiety, obsessive-compulsive concerns and problems on the Autism Spectrum.

Your "bipolar child" is probably extremely precocious, gifted and bright.

I hope they are but of course in life there are no guarantees. We all tend to have our strengths and weaknesses and we all tend to be bored by something. Your child may be smart but bored by the teacher and that may lead to achievement concerns, however that is not always the case. Your child may have ADHD, a Specific Learning Disorder or other problems. If there are problems it is important to have a psychologist or other qualified professional evaluate the child. If things aren't working try another one and keep trying.

The authors of *The Bipolar Child* suggested that parents should judge the professionals they work with by answers to questions like *"Do you strictly adhere to DSM-IV criteria?"* (suggesting it would be bad if they said yes) and *"Is it your observation that symptoms of this illness differ from the adult form...?"* The authors recommend that if the doctor says essentially that they agree with the authors' viewpoint and "...treat this form of the condition as a bipolar disorder anyway, the parents should breathe a sigh of relief." Unfortunately, we now know that what the authors wrote is in general not correct and that their advice can be misleading. Unfortunately, the authors have now actually set up these parents to turn their backs on a more evidence-based approach. The reality is that while the authors tell parents to not seek treatment from anyone that disagrees with the authors, the authors' views do not reflect the current state of the evidence or the current state of the art of treatment. Much of the advice that exists in books like *The Bipolar Child* are now dangerous, outdated jumps-to-conclusion which should be disregarded. My advice is to throw books like *The Bipolar Child* away so that no one accidentally reads them. They should not be seen on your shelf as someone might consider that an implicit recommendation to read the book and trust its contents.

The simplest explanation for why books like *The Bipolar Child* must bend over backwards to try to justify early-onset bipolar and invent new criteria for it is that they've come to the wrong conclusion before all of the evidence was in. The simplest explanation is that arguments for why "early-onset bipolar disorder" is so different from classic bipolar disorder and needs it's own criteria is... that these arguments are even better arguments for why "early-onset bipolar disorder," in most cases, isn't bipolar disorder at all. The arguments for early-onset bipolar disorder needing very different criteria from bipolar disorder are better arguments for it not even being bipolar disorder at all. That is why we now have DMDD under DSM-5.

Disruptive Mood Dysregulation Disorder Diagnostic Criteria

Based on the proposal displayed on the American Psychiatric Association's DSM-5 website April, 2012, the Disruptive Mood Dysregulation Disorder diagnostic criteria will be similar to this. It has not significantly changed according to a personal communication with a work group member (see the recorded Mental Health Day Podcast episode with Dr. Ellen Leibenluft at http://www.mentalhealthday.org). However, since this book went to press prior to the official DSM-5 publication the reader is advised to review the official criteria for diagnostic purposes. The criteria are included here for the dual purposes of scientific commentary and education.

Disruptive Mood Dysregulation Disorder (DMDD):

A. The disorder is characterized by severe, recurrent *temper outbursts* that are grossly out of proportion in intensity or duration to the situation.

> 1. The temper outbursts are manifest verbally and/or behaviorally, such as in the form of verbal rages or physical aggression towards people or property.
>
> 2. The temper outbursts are inconsistent with developmental level.

B. Frequency: The temper outbursts occur, on average, three or more times per week.

C. Mood between temper outbursts:

> 1. Nearly every day, most of the day, the mood between temper outbursts is persistently irritable or angry.
>
> 2. The irritable or angry mood is observable by others (e.g., parents, teachers, peers).

D. Duration: Criteria A-C have been present for 12 or more months.

Throughout that time, the person has not had 3 or more consecutive months when they were without the symptoms of Criteria A-C.

E. Criterion A or C is present in at least two settings (at home, at school, or with peers) and must be severe in at least one setting.

F. The diagnosis should not be made for the first time before age 6 or after age 18.

G. The onset of Criteria A through E is before age 10 years.

H. There has never been a distinct period lasting more than one day during which abnormally elevated or expansive mood was present most of the day, and the abnormally elevated or expansive mood was accompanied by the onset, or worsening, of three of the "B" criteria of mania (i.e., grandiosity or inflated self-esteem, decreased need for sleep, pressured speech, flight of ideas, distractibility, increase in goal directed activity, or excessive involvement in activities with a high potential for painful consequences. Abnormally elevated mood should be differentiated from developmentally appropriate mood elevation, such as occurs in the context of a highly positive event or its anticipation.

I.   The behaviors do not occur exclusively during an episode of Major Depressive Disorder and are not better accounted for by another mental disorder (e.g., Autism Spectrum Disorder, Posttraumatic Stress Disorder, Separation Anxiety Disorder, Dysthymic Disorder). (Note: This diagnosis cannot co-exist with Oppositional Defiant Disorder or Bipolar Disorder, though it can co-exist with Attention Deficit/Hyperactivity Disorder, Conduct Disorder, and Substance Use Disorders. **Individuals meeting criteria for both Disruptive Mood Dysregulation Disorder and Oppositional Defiant Disorder should only be given the diagnosis of Disruptive Mood Dysregulation Disorder.** If an individual has ever experienced a manic or hypomanic episode, the diagnosis of Disruptive Mood Dysregulation Disorder should not be assigned.) The symptoms are not due to the effects of a drug or to a general medical or neurological condition.

Hear more online

I (Dr. Todd Finnerty) interviewed Dr. Ellen Leibenluft on The Mental Health Day Podcast and you may wish to listen to the interview which is available at www.mentalhealthday.org

Do adults have DMDD?

A note about criterion F which states: "The diagnosis should not be made for the first time before age 6 or after age 18." The DSM-5 workgroup reportedly debated this criterion. However, given that there is little research done in adults on DMDD & severe mood dysregulation they chose to be cautious and include this age range only. There is ample research on this group in children but very little in adults. In adults who seem to meet DMDD criteria, for now, other disorders can be considered including Intermittent Explosive Disorder, Personality Disorders, and chronic depressive disorders like Persistent Depressive Disorder (which includes both dysthymia and chronic Major Depressive Disorder from DSM-IV). While a good history is advised and could presumably lead to making the diagnosis in adults over 18, professionals should wait for further research on DMDD in adults. They do not have to diagnose them with Bipolar Disorder, however, when another diagnosis such as a unipolar major depressive disorder or an anxiety disorder may be more appropriate.

As time goes on we may continue to diagnose DMDD much like we diagnose oppositional defiant disorder (ODD).

Professionals tend to not diagnose ODD in adults and instead diagnose these difficulties with a different disorder. However, with more research Criterion F may be changed in future editions of the DSM-5 to allow for DMDD to be diagnosed more like professionals diagnose ADHD. While ADHD was originally considered a childhood problem, it is now also recognized as continuing to create impairment in to adulthood for many people. Some adults now receive an ADHD diagnosis for the first time as an adult.

If professionals take a careful, extensive evaluation they may increasingly recognize DMDD and diagnose it in adults over 18 once the research supports it. However, at this time for DMDD this should be done only in well-controlled research studies. We do not wish to repeat some of our past mistakes of jumping to conclusions before sufficient research is in.

What diagnostic code should Disruptive Mood Dysregulation Disorder be "billed" under?

 DMDD initially shares the same diagnostic code as Mood Disorder NOS (Mood Disorder unspecified) under DSM-5. The American Psychiatric Association must apply to get new codes added to the ICD-9-CM and ICD-10-CM. The American Psychiatric Association will be applying to the ICD-9-CM Coordination and Maintenance Committee to add a new code for DMDD in to the "CM" version of the ICD used in the United States.

The "CM" version of the ICD is a clinical modification from the version of the ICD created by the World Health Organization (WHO). Professionals in the United States must bill with codes from the CM modification of the ICD. Most currently use the DSM to determine how they arrive at ICD codes since the DSM offers guidelines and criteria for deciding which ICD diagnosis code someone has. There are many differences between the WHO's version of the ICD and the "CM" version used in the United States. The WHO is currently working on a new version, the ICD-11, and DMDD may or may not be officially included in the WHO's version. If you'd like to learn more about the relationship between the DSM and the ICD you can do so at www.psychcontinuinged.com

Why does the DSM-5 include DMDD?

Children are not just "little adults." There may in some instances be what some call "developmental manifestations" of bipolar disorder and other problems. This would mean that a disorder might look differently in a person at different points in their developmental lifespan. So at age 7 Bipolar Disorder may look differently than at age 27. However, while children are not little adults they are also not "little lab rats" that clinicians should use untested philosophies and untested treatments on. Many of the proposed approaches that have created "developmental manifestations" of bipolar disorder that were different from the adult criteria have proven to be flawed and potentially harmful to these young children. These poorly tested theories were marketed to the public for use outside of well-designed research studies and took hold among some clinicians before sufficient evidence was available. While we can't treat children like little adults, they also deserve to have approaches developed for them which are helpful and scientifically sound. It is important to review what is and what is not bipolar disorder under DSM-5.

What Changes have been made to Bipolar Disorder in DSM-5?

The DSM-5 has not left bipolar disorder alone. They have made changes, including adding an "anxious distress" specifier that can be used with both bipolar disorders and depressive disorders. Individuals who are diagnosed with bipolar (and unipolar depressive disorders) sometimes also complain of significant symptoms of anxiety as part of their difficulties. Having this significant "anxious distress" presentation alone in addition to a unipolar depression does not mean that that person necessarily has a bipolar disorder.

The revised bipolar disorder criteria also emphasize changes in activity and energy, not just changes in mood, when considering issues like mania and hypomania. Bipolar disorder is not just simply being "moody" and not simply having irritable "mood swings." The DSM-IV definition of a manic episode reflects a distinct period of abnormally and persistently elevated, expansive or irritable mood lasting at least 1 week. The focus on irritability has been reduced in DSM-5.

Differential Diagnosis and Comorbidity: Is it DMDD or bipolar disorder?

About DSM-5 diagnoses

The Diagnostic and Statistical Manual of Mental Disorders (DSM) contains clinical descriptions and diagnostic guidelines to "catalog" problems that mental health professionals treat and also to help improve reliability so that 2 professionals will arrive at the same diagnosis for the same person. The previous edition, the DSM-IV, was not a perfectly valid "bible" and neither is the DSM-5. Another approach, the ICD-11 from the World Health Organization (WHO), will not be perfect either. Other research approaches focusing more on reducing mental illness down to smaller, shared components are a long way off from being useful to clinicians.

The DSM-5 has received plenty of criticism in the media (some of it deserved). Much of the criticism of DSM-5 is also applicable to its predecessor, the DSM-IV. Psychiatric diagnoses at this point are only as valuable as they are useful and lead to helping people. We have not seen a "scientific revolution" with DSM-5. The DSM-5 has resulted only in some "tinkering" of diagnoses, not a major change in how we view psychiatric disorders. Much of what has changed was the result of expert consensus and even the changes should of course not be viewed as gospel. For example, in ADHD the age where we must notice a child has a problem by increased from 7 to 12. Why 12? Ultimately you could ask the same question of why 7? It too was the result of a group of experts coming together to review research and trends and haggle over finding consensus. These experts selected by the American Psychiatric

Association are responsible for the set of diagnoses that made it in to the DSM-5.

No set of diagnoses would perfectly reflect everyone who has problems unless there were almost as many diagnoses as there were people with problems. While we may share some genes, we all have had different experiences and environments and show those genes a bit differently. We have different views of the world, find different ways to cope and each of our skills have developed (or not developed) to varying degrees. Finding a perfect set of diagnostic criteria to describe everyone who needs help is highly improbable. In our lifetimes we also will not achieve a purely biological understanding of how each of us is "programmed" sufficiently to solve the problems of kids with DMDD biologically. The most medications can do at this point is make some of the symptoms less noxious (while introducing the potential for side effects). Some in psychiatry have chosen to focus less on diagnoses themselves and instead focus on symptoms that may be dulled with medication.

While many professionals have grown accustomed to the weaknesses of the DSM-IV and the variety with which their patients present, there can be dangers if we stray too far from good research and established science. That is why while no diagnosis is perfect, it is still valuable, important and meaningful to carefully consider differential diagnoses under DSM-5.

One aspect to consider when deciding whether someone has DMDD or bipolar disorder is family history. Problems like ADHD, bipolar disorder and even depression tend to have genetic components and run in families. If a parent has ADHD their children are more likely to have ADHD. If a close family member has classic bipolar disorder than their children are more likely to have classic bipolar disorder.

The science in regards to DMDD at this point reflects that these children do not grow up to have classic bipolar disorder. In addition, their close family members do not tend to have classic bipolar disorder either (though they do tend to have other problems like unipolar depression, ADHD, etc.). While it is not perfect, attending to family history can be helpful in our approach to these young children with problems. What DMDD children experience is not the same thing as a manic episode, though their outbursts (rages, extreme tantrums, etc.) can be as severe if not more severe than mania. These children have chronic, severe non-episodic irritability and emotional dysregulation.

Fear of harm?
The authors of *The Bipolar Child* have recently begun promoting a *for further*

research syndrome that kids may have that they call bipolar and also label them as having "fear of harm." It's not actually new, it's essentially their same approach to early-onset bipolar disorder. It will be important to continue to monitor any research findings that result from this and whether or not these children are actually similar to others with what we have historically referred to as bipolar disorder (manic depression).

Professionals and parents should remember that while these approaches may be marketed to them on websites, in books and through the media, these alternative approaches to diagnosis and treatment should not be used outside of a well-designed research study. While these authors have promoted the use of drugs like Ketamine for these children before they've even completed any meaningful studies with these children, please remember that professionals should consult the available primary research and not just popular press interviews. This is particularly true with drugs which are not FDA approved for these young children. While these kids, in future research studies, may respond to Ketamine and may have the symptoms described, that still doesn't mean it should be called "juvenile bipolar." In fact, drugs like Ketamine have seen some success with chronic, treatment-resistant unipolar depression.

It is a far greater virtue when it comes to these children to not do harm than to be aggressively and spectacularly wrong. It is important that we continue to evaluate the research evidence and get multiple opinions on it. The research now shows that approaches that prematurely deviated from DSM-IV were wrong. The advice to parents and professionals in books like *The Bipolar Child* is now outdated and is potentially harmful itself.

Changes to ADHD, ODD and other childhood disorders in DSM-5

ADHD

The symptoms of ADHD have remained stable from DSM-IV. A few changes related to diagnosing ADHD are notable with DSM-5, including the removal of "types" in favor of analogous specifiers that mean essentially the same thing. In the future predominately inattentive kids with few hyperactive symptoms who fall in to research categories like "sluggish cognitive tempo" may get more attention, however they do not have their own diagnosis in DSM-5.

Current changes also include allowing adults to be diagnosed with ADHD by meeting fewer criteria than are required in children. This is based on ongoing research in adults with ADHD who continue to show ADHD-related functional impairment but do not necessarily meet all of the relatively child-centric criteria that were in the DSM-IV. The example of ADHD exhibits why it is important to continue to research the diagnostic concepts we use and change our thinking as necessary when research does support new approaches.

In addition, the age of onset of ADHD symptoms has been changed. In DSM-IV the age of onset had relatively arbitrarily been set at age 7. This means to be diagnosed, a child would have to have been observed to have had problems prior to age 7. The DSM-5 now says the child has to have been observed having had problems prior to age 12. This is perhaps a more reasonable boundary relative to childhood. As children approach 12 and beyond however, parents should be aware of an increase in risk for developing mood disorders.

Kids with DMDD are highly likely to also be experiencing ADHD symptoms. In fact, some of the criteria used with the "severe mood dysregulation" research category were taken from ADHD. These criteria were dropped as unnecessary in DSM-5. If a child shows these difficulties they may also potentially qualify for an ADHD diagnosis. DMDD kids may also be experiencing ADHD concerns as well as Specific Learning Disorders and language problems. ADHD can be diagnosed along with DMDD in DSM-5 (however remember that ODD cannot be).

I highly recommend Russell Barkley, Ph.D.'s publications for learning more about ADHD itself. You can learn about them at his website http://www.russellbarkley.org/ I interviewed Dr. Barkley for The Mental Health Day Podcast (you can listen to the interview for free online at www.mentalhealthday.org). There are also 15 academic lectures on ADHD from Dr. Barkley available at www.psychcontinuinged.com.

We often overlook emotions in ADHD (and ODD). However this view is "now changing," according to Dr. Barkley. People with ADHD do have problems with emotional control just as much as they do with other forms of self-control difficulties. Some problems with mood dysregulation could be the impact on executive functioning of ADHD alone. We cannot ignore the emotional component in ADHD. Kids with ADHD do experience trouble controlling their normal emotional responses.

However, ADHD differs from mood disorders and is a neurodevelopmental disorder, not a depressive or bipolar disorder. People with ADHD tend to experience emotions which are normal for the situation, however they have difficulties controlling their strong but normal emotions. They have the same emotions others would have but have less ability to exercise control over their impulses when experiencing them. They show their normal emotions impulsively without good executive control.

Individuals with mood disorders experience emotions that others wouldn't necessarily experience in the given situation, for example a manic episode, prolonged rages or suicidal ideation. They tend to not be consistent with what others would feel in the same situation or are grossly out of proportion or tend to be extreme by comparison.

Oppositional Defiant Disorder & Conduct Disorder

ODD and Conduct Disorder are not necessarily the mild and more severe forms of the same disorder. They are different, though are typically boiled down to "kids with behavior problems." However, kids with ODD often go on to experience depression. Kids with Conduct

Disorder are at higher risk of having Antisocial Personality Disorder as adults.

Under DSM-IV professionals were not allowed to diagnose both ODD and Conduct Disorder at the same time. However, this exclusion criterion has been removed in DSM-5. They can now be considered to have both ODD and Conduct Disorder. Symptoms of ODD in DSM-5 are now grouped in to 3 types: *"angry/irritable mood, argumentative/defiant behavior, and vindictiveness, reflecting that the disorder includes both emotional and behavioral symptoms."*

The DSM-5 workgroup considered placing DMDD kids in a grouping with children who were ODD. However, they believed simply labeling these children with ODD would not get them the access to services that they need. There is a wide-range of severity in the heterogenous (varied) group of kids who meet criteria for ODD.

However, kids who have DMDD tend to have very severe functional impairment and need more help than a diagnosis of ODD would imply. For this reason, if a child meets both the criteria for ODD and for DMDD (which is highly likely), only DMDD is diagnosed as it implies greater severity and a more significant mood component. ODD cannot be diagnosed with DMDD under DSM-5, however conduct disorder can be diagnosed along with DMDD.

"Normal" Temper Tantrums

DMDD can be viewed to some extent as delays in the development of critical skills involved in regulating emotions. These children have significant difficulties which are far beyond what is considered developmentally appropriate. Children cannot be diagnosed with DMDD prior to age 6 and for the most part out of the "preschool years." In a NIMH-funded study it was found that daily tantrums and tantrums with severe behaviors are unusual. In a study of 1,500 preschoolers (3-5) less than 10% of them reportedly had daily temper tantrums. It may be a worse sign if these tantrums come on unpredictable (ex: a parent doesn't know why the child had it or it doesn't occur at a time like nap time or when the child is overwhelmed or hungry). It makes sense for parents and professionals to explore the times when these tantrums have arisen. They can then find ways to prevent them and help the child develop the skills to deal with those situations.

Treatment Options, Measuring Outcomes & Parenting the DMDD child

Go online for more information:
Dr. Todd Finnerty has interviewed internationally known professionals like Dr. Alan Kazdin, Dr. Russell Barkley, Dr. Thomas Phelan and Dr. Ellen Leibenluft for The Mental Health Day podcast. You can listen to those entire interviews and

more online for free right now at
http://www.mentalhealthday.org

There are limitations in our current
research on the treatment of kids meeting
the DSM-5 DMDD criteria. While there
has been research on the similar "severe
mood dysregulation" and early-onset
bipolar disorder concepts, the specific
DMDD criteria are still very new.
However, these childrens' problems are
not new and their parents have been
seeking the help of mental health
professionals for years. They've been
called defiant, moody, sometimes
"bipolar" and have often had multiple
psychiatric diagnoses.

What does good treatment look like in
these children that we now call DMDD?"
It of course begins with a good evaluation
from a competent mental health
professional. It also doesn't hurt to seek a
second opinion. It involves getting
everyone involved in the child's life on a

similar page when possible. This means parents, grandparents, psychologists, school personnel (including teachers and counselors), psychiatrists, pediatricians, etc. This is in part because these problems will not be solved completely by just a pill or even just a once-per-week play therapy session. Approaches to working with children with ADHD, DMDD and similar problems should include "point-of-performance" interventions. That means wherever they are expected to display good behaviors or use good emotional regulation skills ("perform") they should have some assistance or accommodations for the difficulties they experience. This will help them to prevent problems in their natural environment as well as practice and build up these important skill while they are having those demands placed on them at home, school and in the community. Treatment should not be confined to a once-per-week visit to the psychotherapy office. These kids need point-of-performance approaches and not just once-per-week approaches.

For younger children these point-of-performance interventions will most likely include approaches for the parents to try at home. This is usually not because professionals are questioning a caregiver's parenting skills. It is because many of these children can benefit from specialized approaches like those offered through behavioral therapy and parent management training. For older children and teens approaches may include cognitive-behavioral therapy (CBT) homework to be done outside of the therapy session. The research has demonstrated significant improvement with the use of CBT as well as some other forms of psychotherapy.

Additional resources for you to consider include Dr. Russell Barkley's books on ADHD and defiant children. Dr. Thomas Phelan's 1-2-3 Magic books offer good advice, including to stop the extraneous nagging if parents choose to count to 3 when their child misbehaves. Alan Kazdin's "The Kazdin Method for Parenting the Defiant Child" and the collaborative problem solving (CPS) approach described in Dr. Ross Greene's book "The Explosive Child" are also valuable. While the authors of these books may not always agree on everything, they each offer supportable, interesting and important perspectives to dealing with difficult children.

Russell Barkley's books on ADHD and Defiant Children are useful and written by perhaps the most knowledgeable person in the field about ADHD. I highly recommend them, particularly for recommendations specific to children, adolescents and adults with ADHD. http://www.russellbarkley.org/

A word of caution: Dr. Barkley notes that most interventions that are focused on just one small part of a child's life will likely not be particularly successful. As noted, Dr. Barkley indicates that interventions should be at the "point-of-performance." For example, if a child is having trouble in school there is only so far a once-per-week counselor will be able to take a child in addressing that problem unless they also help to intervene in the school setting. Treatment approaches should target all areas where a child is having problems and have interventions designed to occur at the point where the problem occurs. In a school setting parents and professionals can consult with teachers to get their observations about difficulties the child has and also to help monitor the impact of interventions. They can work to create accommodations and ways of working on any difficulties the child may be having in school. Parents should not be blamed for neurodevelopmental disorders like ADHD or language problems or mood disorders. However, the involvement of parents and other caretakers in treatment is critical if these interventions are to be successful. A parent cannot expect to take a child to a psychotherapist once per week, say "fix this," and have the child become instantly better. Parents will need to help craft and monitor these "point-of-performance" interventions that will help children learn to regulate their emotions and their behaviors more adaptively. While it's likely not the "parent's fault" in most of these cases, parents are still on the hook to help find and implement solutions.

Dr. Ross Greene emphasizes intervening proactively before your child has explosive outbursts. He describes a method to help your child practice and develop skills to solve problems and handle frustrations more adaptively. He also describes ways of reducing hostility and antagonism between parents and children. His collaborative problem solving approach offers another perspective that is valuable. Dr. Greene's philosophy is that "kids do well if they can." If a child could do well they would do well. That is why he notes that the most important thing you can do is to try and understand why a child's behavior is rageful and explosive. If, for example, we say it's because the child is a brat and wants to be the boss then our solution is to try to show the child who really is "boss." If we frame the child as having bipolar disorder then our solution is often Lithium or antipsychotic medication without any other interventions at all. If we discover that the child needs help developing skills to regulate their emotions, as Dr. Greene suggests, one potential solution becomes to try to help them find ways of better expressing and regulating their emotions and behaviors.

Dr. Greene suggests that "flexibility, frustration tolerance, and problem-solving are critical developmental skills that some children fail to learn at an age-appropriate pace. Inadequate development of these skills can contribute to a variety of behaviors-outbursts, explosions and physical and verbal aggression." Dr. Greene suggests that a child's "lagging skills" and unsolved problems contribute to their difficulties. He suggests expressing empathy for a child and getting their perspective on the problems leading to the behavior. He suggests helping the child to define the problem, later voicing your concerns and then inviting the child to propose solutions with you to address both the child and the adult's concerns. You can learn more about collaborative problem solving in Dr. Greene's book *The Explosive Child.*

Psychotherapy (including Cognitive-Behavioral Therapy)

CBT is actually a collection of psychotherapeutic approaches, many of which tend to be demonstrated to be effective with difficulties like depression and anxiety. For example, one form of CBT that can be used with PTSD, obsessive-compulsive disorder and anxiety is called prolonged exposure therapy. In general it involves having people face their fears while not allowing them to engage in their compulsive responses. They may engage in more adaptive responses such as relaxation. Another form of CBT is called Dialectical Behavior Therapy (DBT). DBT is an approach used to help patients with pervasive emotional dysregulation, suicidality, and who have often failed at other treatments. It was first developed for chronic suicidal thoughts and was then extended to problems like borderline personality disorder.

Dr. Judith Beck notes that dysfunctional thinking tends to underlie psychological problems. In CBT psychotherapists help people learn to evaluate their thinking in a more realistic and adaptive way. A patient's basic beliefs about themselves, their world and other people will influence their emotions and behaviors. When it comes to children, they are all just beginning in life and just learning how to regulate their emotions and their thoughts effectively. CBT is often noted to be one of the psychotherapeutic approaches that, in general, has some of the most research studies conducted demonstrating it to be effective.

Unfortunately, not all treatment approaches are ideal for all childhood problems. It is important to work with your child's mental health professional to ensure that the treatment approach they are taking is supported by the evidence for their difficulties. When things aren't going well it is important to give that feedback to the mental health professional and work on ways of improving the treatment. They may be able to help with any misunderstandings about implementing point-of-performance interventions including parent management training. They also may be able to offer different approaches themselves or in some circumstances a referral to another provider who can help with other approaches if the current approach is not effective for your child. For example, unstructured play therapy may not always be the most effective approach for certain problems or a specific child. However, in those instances parents could work with their treatment providers to find alternative approaches-- for example Parent Child Interaction Therapy, CBT or Parent Management Training.

Parent Management Training

Many times school teachers, parents and counselors will focus on a child's behavior and create rewards for reducing those behaviors. They may create a chart noting when a child does a behavior that the adult wants or they may even put checkmarks next to their name if they've done something undesirable. Dr. Alan Kazdin notes that these reward charts are a "very tiny part" of an effective behavior management program. Dr. Kazdin notes that these reward charts are often "more for the parent" to help them structure the program and stay with it themselves.

One suggestion Dr, Kazdin has for tantrums is to help the child practice "good tantrums" under simulated conditions where the child doesn't engage in unwanted behavior. The child is given opportunities to repeatedly practice a better way of dealing with emotions. Parents should praise in a special kind of way: effusively, specifically, and with a nonverbal pat on the shoulder or other touch. Repeated practice and rewards encourage the desired behaviors to occur again in the future.

When there is something negative you want to get rid of, we have to "attend to the positive opposite" according to Dr. Kazdin. We focus on and reward the desired behaviors and desired ways of dealing with our emotions. Learn more from Dr. Kazdin at http://childconductclinic.yale.edu/ and http://www.alankazdin.com/

It is important to keep track of successes and difficulties. We can use a reward chart for this, however parents, children and teens can potentially keep a mood diary or mood chart. There are mood charts that are available for free on the internet but parents and professionals may also wish to work with the child to tailor their own that is specific to the problems the child is having and wants to work on.

Medications
The authors of *The Bipolar Child* give "toxic advice." While the authors of *The Bipolar Child* repeatedly caution against antidepressants and stimulants in favor

of mood stabilizers, they also characterize ECT as a "safe option" that is "unsurpassed by any other treatment in psychiatry." While certainly these treatment approaches may be indicated in some instances, they should not be considered first-line treatments in these children. Parents and professionals must be aware of the potential that antidepressants may impact suicidality and lead to a manic episode. However, parents and professionals should weigh the risks of the rare child who will actually have a manic episode to the more likely risks of putting many more children on more toxic medications with worse side effects. The authors of *The Bipolar Child* jump to the wrong conclusion and suggest jumping to more toxic medications. A good, evidence-based evaluation can help to determine the extent of risk for an actual manic episode. In addition, psychotherapy and point-of-performance interventions are an effective alternative to these more toxic medications for many kids who meet criteria for DMDD.

Unfortunately, the authors of *The Bipolar Child* do not appear to be very familiar with non-medication, psychosocial approaches. Better, "less toxic" advice is not simply shunning less toxic medications like antidepressants and stimulants immediately in favor of medications which aren't even FDA approved for use in children. Better, "less toxic" advice is to get a good, thorough workup from a qualified professional and a second opinion. I will show my bias as a psychologist here and suggest that parents also go to a child psychologist. Psychologists and other mental health professionals have other effective, non-medication interventions at their disposal.

When it comes to DMDD we should not ignore the power of psychosocial interventions delivered by psychologists and other mental health professionals. Psychotherapy and working with important people in the child's life to set up point-of-performance interventions should be considered the first line treatment for DMDD. Medications may of course be necessary and useful for kids with DMDD. While care should be taken in children at risk for mania, less toxic medications like antidepressants and stimulants should not be immediately ruled out in these kids. If the predominant problem is irritability and there is no clear evidence of classic manic episodes parents and professionals should be very skeptical about the "toxic advice" from books like *the Bipolar Child.* If you know of parents adhering to books like *The Bipolar Child* as though they were a "bible" on these kids, please spread the word about DMDD and that there may be alternatives for their children.

The research shows that most of these kids do not share the same qualities as kids and adults who do have a bipolar disorder. Much of the advice in books like *The Bipolar Child* should now be viewed as simply wrong and frankly dangerous. Parents and professionals should not just jump straight to the most toxic classes of medications as though they were the first line of treatment when these children likely do not have a bipolar disorder.

Before DSM-5 there was no good "diagnostic home" for these kids. However, now we can diagnose most of what used to be considered "early-onset bipolar" as the unipolar mood disorder Disruptive Mood Dysregulation Disorder. Psychologists and other mental health professionals have effective approaches for these kids and with the new DMDD diagnosis we will be able to continue to refine our approach to best meet their needs.

For Further Reading- Parents

Websites
Check out our website and subscribe to DMDD news updates at www.disruptivemooddysregulation.com

Listen to Dr. Finnerty interview interesting people on mental health related topics for free at http://www.mentalhealthday.org

Books to check out

The Kazdin Method for Parenting the Defiant Child by Alan Kazdin

The Explosive Child by Ross Greene

1-2-3 Magic: Effective Discipline for Children 2-12 by Thomas Phelan

Taking Charge of ADHD, Revised Edition: The Complete, Authoritative Guide for Parents by Russell Barkley

Book to throw away:
The Bipolar Child: The Definitive and Reassuring Guide to Childhood's Most Misunderstood Disorder by Demitri Papolos, M.D. and Janice Papolos

For Further Reading- Professionals

Websites
Get continuing education credits for reading this book at www.psychcontinuinged.com

Listen to Dr. Finnerty interview interesting people on mental health related topics for free at http://www.mentalhealthday.org

Books to check out:

Parent Management Training by Alan Kazdin

Defiant Children: A Clinician's Manual for Assessment and Parent Training, Third Edition by Russell Barkley

Book to throw away:
The Bipolar Child: The Definitive and Reassuring Guide to Childhood's Most Misunderstood Disorder by Demitri Papolos, M.D. and Janice Papolos

Subscribe to DMDD news today
FOR FREE

www.disruptivemooddysregulation.com/DMDDnews

to get occasional news, resources and updates about topics related to Disruptive Mood Dysregulation Disorder sent directly to your email from Todd Finnerty, Psy.D.

Follow **@DrFinnerty** on Twitter

Thank you!

NOTES:

Printed in Great Britain
by Amazon

69177977R00047